"How Did I Get Here?"

Sandy Thrush

Just-For-Fun Publishing, LLC
Kentwood, Michigan
~2008~

How Did I Get Here? © 2008 by Sandy Thrush

Published by: Just-For-Fun Publishing,
PO Box 888162, Kentwood, MI 49588-8162.

Print production by: Central Plains Book
A Division of Sun Graphic, Arkansas City, KS

Cover production by: Sadie Cross, BRIOprint, LLC, Minneapolis, MN

Just-For-Fun Publishing books may be purchased in bulk for educational, business, fundraising, or sales promotional use. For information, please email sandy@justforfunpublishing.com or visit our web site at www.justforfunpublishing.com.

Scripture quotations used in this book are from *The Holy Bible*, The Bible in Basic English, World English Bible, New King James Authorized Version, The Webster Bible Translation, and the NIV Translation from www.CrossDaily.com, online Bible Search.

Words from songs used by permission:

Keep Holding On
Words & music by David Elchler & Kevin Shorey
Fresh Rain Productions,
A division of Lowell Lundstrom Ministries.

I Can Begin Again
Writer Credits: Dave Clark / Larnelle Harris
© 1989 First Row Music/John T. Benson Publishing Co. Inc/Bridge Building

I Can Not Hide From You PR060408-5
Writer Credits: Tony Wood / Scott Krippayne / Steven Rimmon Siler
© New Spring Publishing, Inc./Word Music, LLC ©2003 Silerland Music(Admin. By Word Music, LLC/All Rights Reserved

ISBN 978-0-9821371-1-6

Table of Contents

Foreword

" For I know the plans I have for you," declares the Lord, "Plans to prosper you and not to harm you, plans to give you hope and a future.

Then you will call upon Me and come and pray to Me, and I will listen to you. You will seek Me and find Me when you seek Me with all your heart."

Jeremiah 29:11-13 NIV

I do not remember when I first read this verse in the Bible. But I am sure that I probably just flew by it. I was probably trying to get in my daily quota of reading, and it went in one eye and out the other! I may have even read it several times, and I am sure heard it preached on numerous occasions: in one ear, out the other.

I do remember the day that I *saw* it for the first time. The day the words caught in my throat, blurred in my vision, and burned in my heart. I had, yet again, let sin into my life and plunged rebelliously ahead, to try and get what I wanted, what I deserved, even if it was not what God wanted for me. I wanted it, and that was all that mattered.

But God, in His unending mercy and love, would not let me have my own way. As I stood in frustration and shame, hurting and desperate, I opened my Bible and the above passage was the first thing I saw.

I must have read it through a dozen times. It slowly burned its way into my heart and into my understanding. Regret threatened to overwhelm me. It was reassuring that God had *good* plans for me, but humiliating that I could disregard this fact, once again, and try to push through my own agenda.

I am so thankful for God's unending mercy and love, that He is a God of *second* chances. In my case, second, third and even fourth! That He loves me so much, He stubbornly refuses to allow me to have what I *think* is good for me, and is slowly showing and teaching me to wait on His *good and perfect* plan, in His good and perfect time.

It is funny, but true, hindsight can sometimes give us 20/20 vision. God will reveal our errors to us, but unless we choose to see them, we can go round and round that same mountain and may even remain deluded till we die. More commonly, we tend to see MORE of what really happened as we look back. Often the past is only gradually revealed to us and sometimes not at all if we choose to stubbornly remain blind, keeping our eyes and heart closed to the truth about others and ourselves. Looking back, I can now see the mistakes I made; the wrong turns I took; the foolish choices I made. Again, I cannot stress enough how grateful I am for God's unending mercy and love. Unfortunately, while God grants us forgiveness and restores us, there are still consequences for those choices.

The following pages and chapters are my reflective journey to understanding "How Did I Get Here?" and the things I have learned on this journey. My prayer is that, as you read this, you will maybe be able to avoid some of the pitfalls I jumped into head first, and come to realize just how loving a God we have; and that by truly seeking Him, through His Word and prayer, you can experience the truth of Jeremiah 29:11-13.

God Bless!!!

Sandy

Chapter 1

The Darkness Comes

Being raised by godly parents does not guarantee that a person will make good choices. It does not guarantee a relationship with God. As individual people we go along on the ride of life, thinking everything is just fine and yet we can somehow be totally blind to the attacks of Satan. We walk as close to the fire as possible, all the while trying not to get burned. Each time we "sin" a little and excuse it away, we become more callous, less sensitive to the Holy Spirit trying to guide us back to where God wants us to be. We can be so caught up in "life" that we do not even know that we have become "sick" and need the healing touch of Jesus Christ in our life.

In the summer of 1987, while driving home from a computer class I was taking, I finally took a long cold hard look at myself in the mirror of life and asked myself the question, "How did I get here? When I was walking the pathway of my life, what side road did I take; what choices did I make that brought me to THIS?" I did not have an answer. Because I did not know how I had got to where I was, I did not know how to get back.

That summer my husband and I were working different shifts. He was on first shift, and I worked second. Most of our married life had been littered with, what I felt, was inappropriate behavior, probably not unlike many other couples. You know, that secret side of our lives that we keep discretely hidden. My own feelings of guilt over these activities contributed to the deterioration of not only my feelings of self worth, but also my spiritual, emotional, and physical well-being.

I knew there were serious problems with our marriage, our relationship as husband and wife. The problems we were facing are never just one person's fault. I had no idea what he was feeling because we didn't talk. I only knew what I felt. I felt like he was trying to exercise complete control over our lives. It seemed like he had to control every aspect of not only his life, but also the kids and mine. Little things like not wanting me to get the mail out of the mail box or not wanting me to write checks only made me feel more and more unsure of myself. I had gained a lot of weight and I was very self-conscious of what I thought was him keeping track of every thing I ate. More and more I felt that I could not do enough around the house, and what I did was never good enough. I have a name for this kind of thinking now; it's called "stinkin-thinkin". I couldn't read his mind, so I didn't really know what he was thinking, but it was what I felt.

As I was driving in the car that day, I stared at the truck in front of me. There was a long pole sticking out of the back of the truck with a red flag on the end. I thought, "Just don't step on the brake."

When the realization hit me of what I had just thought about doing, I slammed on the brakes almost getting rear-ended by the car behind me. I sat there, shaking, unable to stop crying, with the man behind me shaking his fist (and finger) at me and saying God knows what. I knew that I needed to tell someone how I was feeling. I needed to get some help. The question was whom could I talk to? Who could I trust?

It is one thing to suddenly realize that your life is in a total downward spiral; out of control; headed for disaster; that you have some real problems; that something desperately needs to change; and quite another to really desire to change things; to be healed; to be forgiven. That is where all change and healing really begins, with the acknowledgement of our sin, our shortcomings, and then true repentance. I say true repentance because just saying you are sorry is not repentance.

True repentance means you look at your sin and honestly call it what it is. There is genuine sorrow for that sin, which leads to a change of heart, which in turn causes us to turn from sin to God. This is the sanctification process of salvation. This repentance from sin plus faith in Christ and all He is and can do in our lives is our human responsibility in the salvation plan. And the sanctification part of salvation *is a process.* In Philippians 2:12 & 13, Paul is writing to the Philippians about the obligations of the Christians.

"So then, my beloved, even as you have always obeyed, not only in my presence, but now much more

in my absence, work out your own salvation with fear and trembling.
For it is God who works in you both to will and to work, for his good pleasure." World English Bible

Too many times we are truly unrepentant. We are only sorry for the consequences of our sins. This sorrow does not bring about a change of heart and without a change of heart we only have a frustrated, angry, painful and guilt-filled life to look forward to here on earth, and separation from God for eternity.

I knew my life was a mess. I wanted things to be different, but I did not want to have to change myself too much. I was hurting and I wanted comfort more than a solution, because a solution would require too much from me. We do a lot of things to fool ourselves into thinking we are trying to do something right, when we are really doing the opposite. It is funny, if you broke your arm, you would never go to a dentist to get it fixed. The same is true when you have a broken spirit, when your soul is sick and needs to be fixed. Up to that point in my life, I had made a lot of bad choices and I made another when I went to a person for help instead of God.

I went to my family physician because I did not know whom else to go to. I had been having trouble sleeping and was feeling sick every time I ate. I was babysitting during the day, besides taking care of our own children and keeping house. I was also taking a computer class three times a week in the afternoon. On my one night off from work I went to a Sign Language class. I worked six days a week and I was learning three new skills at my job. On top of all this, I was drinking a lot of alcohol. I would stay out with the girls I worked with after work, sometimes till after midnight and drink, until I did not feel the fear and frustration in my heart and mind. I realize now I was in major burnout at the time.

When the doctor started asking me questions, I started crying and could not stop. I told him about the episode with the truck and he immediately put me on some diet pills, ("speed" that was legal back in 1987) to give me a little energy and set me up with an appointment with a psychologist. I saw the psychologist, who showed great compassion but immediately steered me toward trying to discover what had happened to me to make me have such low self-esteem. I mean, obviously, someone had *done* something to me to make me feel this way. Whose fault was it that my life was so messed up? Certainly not mine!

Chapter 2

The Journey Down Memory Lane

Even though parents who loved God and truly loved me brought me up in a Christian home, our family was not without their own problems. My parents had up and down times. Their communication skills were not very effective; which resulted in a lot of verbal fighting. Dad was driven by his need to tell others of God's love and Jesus' saving and healing power. However, my Dad was not a Christian when he met my Mother.

They met on a blind date. He was smitten, but she would not agree to see him again. He was very persistent so she agreed to let him come to church with her. He sat with her in a service and was convinced that mom had told the preacher all about him. But how could she? She didn't even know him. He knew at once that it was God who was reaching out to him. He was an alcoholic and chain cigarette smoker, who upon his conversion never took another drink or smoked another cigarette. God miraculously healed him. Because of that, he had a driving desire to tell everyone they are not hopelessly stuck in their sick sin-filled life style. Jesus could and would set them free.

Mom, on the other hand, had been sickly all her life. She was used to people focusing on and meeting her needs, so that is where her focus was.

Do not get me wrong, I had really good parents who loved me and tried very hard to shelter me. But like any married couple they had their share of ups and downs. They made mistakes, but I know they did the best they could. Young children, and even older children, do not know how to process the *down times*. Many times they take on the responsibility of those down times. Looking back now, I have a lot more compassion and understanding of my parents than I did at that time.

No matter how hard you try to protect your children and try to keep them safe, sometimes-bad things happen to them. At the tender age of five, two neighbor boys who were brothers, six and eight years older than I, repeatedly molested me. I never told anyone until years later because they said I would burn in hell if I did. Their older sister somehow discovered that something was going on and threatened to tell my Dad if I ever *did that again*. She said I was a nasty, dirty little girl who was not going to go to heaven when I died. A scary thought to a five year old.

When I was six years old in the first grade, I was punished by a teacher for talking to a boy who sat behind me. He would poke me repeatedly with a pencil, so I finally turned around and asked him to stop. I received a spanking from the teacher. She had me pull my panties down and bend over, standing on a chair in front of the window looking out over the playground. The entire class was standing outside the window watching.

I was in the 3rd grade when the husband of our caregiver molested me. It was our *special time* and no one was to know. I still remembered what the sister of the two brothers had said when I was five. I did not want to burn in hell. I grew up feeling dirty, unworthy of love and stupid. I learned early how to separate myself from reality when it became too painful to face what was going on around me, by creating a make-believe world where I was safe, loved, and everything was wonderful. The problem with that world was it was not real – could never be real – and it only made everything worse.

It is funny, or really not so funny, but once you are abused, somehow it just keeps on happening over and over. It is almost like that pattern gets started, and you become susceptible to that type of behavior from other people. And no matter how terrible it may be, it is something familiar. Each time it happens, you just close your mind a little more until it is something happening to you - but not really. Maybe people who end up abusing other people can somehow sense that in a person, I do not know; but the abuse to me continued into my adult life through many different sources ending up with the hurtful relationship I had with my husband.

I did not tell you all of this to get you to feel sorry for me. I do not know what demons, if any, from your past may be tormenting you, but I do know how horrible demons can be. I want you to know that God is bigger than our past, and you do not have to face anything alone. But you do have to truly desire to face the past and be set free through the power of Jesus Christ, or you will spend the rest of your life putting a bandage over a festering wound that will never heal.

Maybe you are thinking, "Why would anyone not desire to be healed?" Believe it or not, there are benefits in being afflicted. A person can become so accustomed to coping with the disadvantages of afflictions that those disadvantages eventually seem comfortable, even desirable. I think they also become safe. They are safe because they are what we know. The *known* is much safer than the *unknown*. You are used to that whole package--know exactly what to expect--no surprises. Also, healing would mean becoming responsible for our own decisions and the products of our life, and what we have done with our life. Once we are healed, we would no longer have an excuse for not leading a more productive life--it would mean a drastic change in our lifestyle.

Sometimes, it is easier to cling to emotional wounds, whether they are deserved (the consequences of past sins) or undeserved (things done to us), than to face the feelings that are the result of wounding experiences. I think there is a fear that facing true feelings will be too much to handle. Or, maybe it is easier to believe that present misery is deserved payment for past sins, and then we reject accepting God's forgiveness. I mean, if I can accept God's forgiveness of my sin, I will then forgive myself, and the other person/persons involved with the wounding.

I think this is where self-pity comes into play--a great tool of Satan by the way. Most people would rather nurse a grudge against the offending person--make them pay and keep everyone reminded of how bad we were treated. Sometimes we become so used to living with hurt and pain that we are afraid to live without it. That brings us right back to the fact that if we are healed from an emotional wound, there is no longer an excuse to keep us from being more responsible and living a more productive life. That is an unknown, and therefore it holds the possibility of failure. But the alternative to not truly being healed is to never be able to move on, to do—to be—all that God has planned for your life. That would be a tragic loss.

One thing I learned through all of this: no matter how I feel, or what has happened to me in the past, I - and only I - am responsible for what I do. The bad choices I made, for whatever reason, were still made by me. Please understand - my parents, my sister, and my extended family - they all loved me very much. I just had too many secrets and too much shame I could not process. It was easier to pretend than to face any of it, and later, to accept my own responsibility for the choices I made after an offence or wounding incident.

I told myself that I wanted to be good. I loved God. After all, I had asked Jesus into my heart. I was a Christian. But when situations arose that I could not deal with, instead of turning to Jesus, I would react in human fashion, and then because of shame I would deny to myself that I had reacted that way. I would go off into a fantasy. Before long I was not able to discern what was real and what was make-believe. Philippians 4:8 says:

> **"Finally, brothers, whatever things are true, whatever things are honorable, whatever things are just, whatever things are pure, whatever things are lovely, whatever things are of good report; if there is any virtue, and if there is any praise, think about these things."**
> **World English Bible**

Long after I stopped going to the psychologist this verse came to my attention and Jesus was finally able to start working on my sick and broken spirit with me. I say He worked *with* me because that is really the first step that has to be taken to receive healing; realizing that time and effort are involved in the healing, and that I have to be active in that healing process. Sometimes we are so distracted by all the pain and fear involved, God has to allow something drastic to get our attention and involvement.

Like I said, I wanted the pain to stop, but I did not want to have to change me too much. I did one day say a simple prayer. I was kind of playing at changing a little, and had started going to a Bible study about prayer, so I said to God, "I don't always make the right choice, and things are kind of messed up in my life right now, so maybe, instead of me making decisions, You could. I give up my right to choose - I give that right to You. I am asking You to make sure I do not screw up and end up in hell." Sometimes, to really be healed, God has to let us go all the way down, flat on our face. That is exactly what happened to me. My whole world fell apart. When that happened, the only way I could look was up, back to Him.

Chapter 3

Wrong Turns

Because I was going over all the past things that had happened to me, things that had been *done to me*, and everything I had done after the fact, the conclusion I came to in processing all this was, that nothing was my fault. There was no accountability on my part, no repentance, no acknowledgement of or accountability for my own actions, and therefore no forgiveness. I could not or would not accept my own responsibility, so I could not forgive myself, and I grew more and more depressed. My first suicide attempt put me in the hospital for two weeks. I'm sure now that this action on my part hurt my husband's pride, and I believe that it also made him angry.

I have already talked a little about the condition of our marriage. I believe that it lacked the foundation of God's ideals and principles, and I knew it was failing. I was terrified of the possibility of divorce. I had always thought that divorce was a terrible sin, and that God would not love me if I got divorced. Besides, what would everyone think? It would hurt and shame my parents. I could not make it better, no matter how hard I tried. You have to know what is wrong before you can fix something, and I did not have a clue.

Did I ask God to help me fix my failing marriage? I have to now say no. I do not believe you can call crying and begging God to fix something as really asking God for help. God does not just wave some magic wand and make everything better. Do I believe God will not listen when we cry out to Him? No. I know He hears. However, I do believe if we do not have a truth based intimate relationship with God it can be difficult to really communicate, to hear and understand Him when He is trying to show us the answer, and help us see what our part needs to be in the healing process. Like I said earlier, God will reveal our errors to us, but unless we choose to see them, if we choose to stubbornly remain blind, keeping our eyes and heart closed to the truth about others and ourselves, we can go round and round that same mountain and may even remain deluded till we die. He will show us the answer, but we have to truly want to see it.

I am convinced that to repair a failing marriage requires a tremendous amount of work on the part of both people. They have to both want to make it work for anything to be accomplished. I will be honest, my first attempt at suicide was a form of manipulation -- to try and *make* my husband change the way he felt toward me. I hoped to make him want to stay with me; to make him love me the way God intended a man to love his wife. I thought I could make him love me by my needing him to protect me, to keep me safe, to get me well.

The opposite happened. My *sickness* and my attempted manipulation only contributed to the widening rift that was developing between us, making him angry and wounding his pride. I actually made it easier for him to divorce me, gain custody of our children and home, and literally put me out on the street. Paperwork was filed to declare me "disabled" and after a second emotional breakdown I was court-committed to a state mental hospital. When he filed for divorce, thereby getting custody of our children and possession of our home, my world came crashing down around my feet.

That is another hard lesson I learned. You cannot *make* someone love you. All you can do is be someone who is loveable. The rest is up to them.

I said earlier that I had asked myself the question, "How Did I Get To This Point in My Life?" Well, I met my husband at state college. That was *Mistake #2*. Do not misunderstand me; there is nothing wrong with a state college. But I knew that God wanted me to go to a Christian College. I had felt that God was calling me into some form of ministry. But in my last year of high school I silently started to rebel. That was *Mistake #1*. 1 Samuel 15:23 says,

> **"For rebellion [is as] the sin of witchcraft, and stubbornness [is as] iniquity and idolatry."**
> **The Webster Bible Translation**

I started smoking and listening to rock music, (really big sins back then) and I decided I was NOT going to become a preacher's wife. There was just too much heartache associated with the job. Besides, I did not deserve anything good - who would want me? Satan is so good at making us feel sorry for ourselves, and for all the wrong choices that we make, giving us excuses. He is not called the father of all lies for nothing. So, I placed myself in a position where I was set up to fall.

When I first met my husband, I did not know that he did not believe in God. He did not swear, smoke, or drink – you know, all those things we call *sin*. When I found out I was devastated. I said I could not see him any more. It had been drilled into me from a very young age – be not unequally yoked together with unbelievers. But he still wanted to see me. I said he could go to church with me. So he did. He told me right off that he would only be going to church with me to be with me, and not because he *believed*. How romantic - the same way my parents got together. I was determined to *save* him. You see, even though I was sowing my own wild oats, I still thought my relationship with God was OK. Deep inside I really did want to walk with God, but on my own terms.

I do believe my husband actually had a salvation experience, but like the parable of the sower in Matthew 13:5-7; 20-22:

"Some fell upon stony places, where they had not much earth: and forthwith they sprung up, because they had no deepness of earth; and when the sun was up, they were scorched, and because they had no root, they withered away. And some fell among thorns; and the thorns sprung up, and choked them....but he that received the seed into stony places, the same is he that hearth the word, and with joy receiveth it; yet hath he not root in himself, but indureth for a while: for when tribulation or persecution ariseth because of the world, by and by he is offended. He also that received seed among the thorns is he that heareth the word; and the care of this world, and the deceitfulness of riches, choke the word, and he becometh unfruitful."
New King James

I have accepted my part in this also. I know my personal up and down walk with the Lord was not a good example. But I can only take so much responsibility for him.

13

He also had God's Word. Whatever I was doing, he still had his own decisions and choices to make. Right from the start we did not follow God's plans.

Right from the start our relationship was a very physical one. When we got married, I did not know if he really loved me and I was not even sure if I loved him. Since we had been intimate I thought I had to marry him or God would look upon me as a fornicator. The truth is, I was a fornicator. Marrying him did not change that. I do not know why I thought it would. Now it's obvious it was another lie from Satan. Are you beginning to see the pattern here? If we let him, Satan will whitewash every obvious sin. Here's another lie: Everyone's doing it these days.

Mistake #3: We lived together prior to being married. Looking back on that time, I can see how that decision changed both of us. We lost the innocence, the pureness, the expectancy and anticipation of new young love. More than ever I now believe that without a non-physical relationship, and a foundation based on God's values and moral guidelines, the possibility of that relationship lasting a life time, through good and bad times is slim to none.

Mistake #4 was going ahead with the marriage when I had strong doubts about our relationship, and something happened that made me think that God did not want me to marry him. On our wedding day, as I stood with my dad waiting to walk down the isle, I heard a voice say out loud; **"What are you doing marrying this man--you do not know him."** I remember asking my dad if he had said something. He replied he had not. To this day I believe it was God. I know now that I could have told my dad that I had already made one mistake, and that I did not want to make it worse by marrying someone that maybe I was not suppose to marry. I know now that he would have stood by my side and whisked me out of there and he would have helped me to get back on the right path. Even at that point in my life I could have started over, but I let pride keep me from acknowledging my sin. Instead I held on to Satan's lie about my sin and plunged stubbornly and rebelliously ahead to do what I wanted to do.

I need to say right here, that if my husband and I had truly put God first in our lives and repented of our sin, God

14

could have made our marriage a good one and we could have gone on in His will from that point. Instead, our marriage was a roller coaster of selfishness and hurtful actions on both our parts. We also went from one religion to another, one denomination to another; always looking for something that would make us feel good about ourselves without having to change ourselves too much.

In all of this, God did bless us with two beautiful children. I am truly thankful for both of them.

By the time I had reached the point of the beginning of this story, my husband was so involved in his work, and I was feeling so worthless, overwhelmed, and out of touch with reality that I was convinced that I could not live the lifestyle I felt he wanted from me and so I believed that I was more of a problem for him than someone he wanted to love and share a life with. Added to this was Satan showing his true colors by whispering in my ear how I was going to be punished for all my sins and that I was going to get what I deserved.

I truly believe that when we open the door to ungodly counsel, we open the door to demonic oppression, and Satan was definitely oppressing me. I was to a point in my counseling with the psychologist where I was convinced that I had other personalities that were "making" me do things.

I want to take just a moment here to try and explain what the definition of DID/MPD, Dissociative Identity Disorder / Multiple Personality Disorder is. Webster's Ninth New Collegiate Dictionary © 1988 by Merriam-Webster Inc. states:

multiple personality n (1901): an hysterical neurosis in which the personality becomes dissociated into two or more distinct but complex and socially and behaviorally integrated parts each of which becomes dominant and controls behavior from time to time to the exclusion of the others.

Psychology Today from the Internet gives this definition:

Dissociative Identity Disorder (DID) is a severe condition in which two or more distinct identities, or personality states are present in -- and alternately take control of -- an individual. The person also experiences

15

memory loss that is too extensive to be explained by ordinary forgetfulness. The disturbance is not due to the direct psychological effects of a substance or of a general medical condition. DID was called Multiple Personality Disorder until 1994, when the name was changed to reflect a better understanding of the condition -- namely, that it is characterized by a fragmentation, or splintering, of the identity rather than by a proliferation, or growth, of separate identities.

DID reflects a failure to integrate various aspects of identity, memory and consciousness in a single multidimensional self. Usually, a primary identity carries the individual's given name and is passive, dependent, guilty and depressed. When in control, each personality state, or alter, may be experienced as if it has a distinct history, self-image and identity. The alters' characteristics -- including name, reported age and gender, vocabulary, general knowledge, and predominant mood -- contrast with those of the primary identity. Certain circumstances or stressors can cause a particular alter to emerge. The various identities may deny knowledge of one another, be critical of one another or appear to be in open conflict.*

Almost all of us have experienced at one time or another in our life a feeling of detachment or even a sense of separation from our self. Reality can actually stay intact; in that you know what is happening, to a certain degree, but you don't feel like you're the one experiencing it. It's like it's happening to someone else. Most of the time this is the case. More simply stated: denial that we are doing or feeling what ever we may be doing or feeling.

DID/MPD supporters believe that other times, when trauma or abuse is a key factor, a person will have two or more distinct identities, each with its own unique way of relating to the world and to their self. Usually, at least two of these identities recurrently take control of the person's behavior. Frequently there is an inability of the person to recall important personal information to an extent that is more than ordinary forgetfulness. Some classic examples are finding new clothes in your closet which you don't remember buying, finding yourself in a place or situation and not being able to remember how you got there and having a

http://www.psychologytoday.com/conditions/did.html

complete loss of memory for what happened in the previous few hours to days to even weeks and months.

Which of these two scenarios was my case? The fracturing of my personality, or my refusal to admit I was making bad choice or feeling angry and frustrated, I'm not sure. There are large gaps in my memory, but weather I truly had DID/MPD, I do not know. One thing I do know is that the council I was receiving was ultimately providing me with the excuse to be totally unaccountable for my choices and behavior.

Nothing I did was my fault, nor was I accountable for what I was doing. I constantly thought about dying. I held on to just enough of my faith in God to beg Him to please make my husband change his behavior and to not divorce me. Even though our marriage had been a roller coaster of hurt emotions, pain and fear, I did not want a divorce because I felt that would be the ultimate failure. I begged God to let me have my children back, to not send me to hell, to make everything right. All the while I continued to listen to my psychologist and believe that I had no responsibility in all of this. I was a victim of past abuse. In some respects I was. But despite that I was still responsible for my own choices.

Chapter 4

Flat On My Face

When the divorce was final I sunk into even deeper depression. My life was over; my husband was gone, preparing to marry someone else. My children were with him. I had limited visitation. Everyone thought I was mentally ill. I was on disability and welfare and so many different medications, that half the time I did not know what I was doing. But God knew where I was. When my psychologist admitted me to the psychiatric wing of the hospital for the third time it was because she was convinced I was going to kill myself.

I was put on what is called a suicide watch. Every 15 minutes a nurse would come and check on me. I just sat in my room on the bed. I was at a point where I was so heavily medicated that I talked to myself a lot. I existed in a constant state of hallucination.

That February in 1989, as I sat on the side of my bed, my sister and her family were just getting home from church. She felt a strong urgency to pray for me. So my sister, her husband and the kids got down on their knees in the living room and started to pray. They did not stop until she felt a release. At that same time, back in the psychiatric ward of the hospital, I was hallucinating.

I seemed to be floating above my bed. I could see myself sitting on the bed. I watched the nurse come in and check on me and then leave. I saw myself stand up, tie one end of a gown around my neck, walk over to a trash can, turn it over, step up on it, tie the other end of the gown to the cupboard door hinge and then kick the trash can out from under my feet.

I remember thinking the whole time that I was fantasizing – I was not really doing it. But I was. Remember Philippians 4:8? I was not guarding my thoughts. I was letting Satan control me. He almost succeeded in getting me to end my life. It amazes me just how much God loves me. He would not let my sister rest until the danger was past. Just as I kicked the trash can over, the nurse looked up from the desk and saw me.

The staff got to me in time to save my life but not

19

before I had succeeded in almost hanging myself, which did result in a very mild stroke. But God is so merciful. He keeps reaching out to us. The knowledge that I had almost succeeded in ending my life and how much God cared for me by using my sister and her family to intercede for me, right at the exact time it was all happening, made me stop what I was doing and start to take a look at where I was. Oh, everything did not miraculously get better. My ex-husband still remarried -- and not to me. He retained custody of the kids. But I started to turn around. You see, God did not leave me, I had left Him; He did not move, I did.

It is kind of strange how you can hear things that sound good, but they are not "right". My psychologist said just enough good-sounding things - I had a hard time realizing that I was listening to the wrong voice. It was a slow process of breaking away from my psychologist. I still could not admit my own shortcomings and sin and need for repentance and change. Getting all the medication out of my system was very hard. For one thing, the doctors that were treating me were insisting that I continue with the medication even when I did not want to take it. I was trying to get back to God, but I was trying to also stay as close to that old worldly system as I could without actually "being a sinner."

I finally reached a point where I was reading my Bible, and praying, EVERY DAY thinking, "Surely, God will now fix everything because I am being so good." I was doing all the motions, but the true and total giving over control to God had not happened. The true repentance I talked about earlier; the one that brings about a change of heart; had not happened yet. I was *doing* everything I thought I was supposed to do, but I did not *feel* anything. I had a form of godliness, but I was denying the awesome power of God.

Where was God? Was He punishing me for trying to kill myself? Had I committed the *"unpardonable"* sin? Was I going to go through the rest of my life by myself, without my kids, and not even be able to feel God? Always wondering if He had forgiven me? Not knowing for sure if I was going to heaven or hell? Once again, Satan convinced me that I could not expect to know if God would forgive me or not. Why did I think I deserved anything? I decided I could not go on. I went to church one Sunday morning for the last time. I told

God, "This is it, if I can not know that You have forgiven me and love me, I would rather be dead." That was the morning that Kevin Shorey, a Christian singing artist, was visiting and got up and sang, "Keep Holding On".

"You're surrounded by the night,
you've lost your will to fight,
there's no way out so it seems.
Ya say there's no hope,
you're at the end of your rope,
your life is nothin' but shattered dreams.
If mistakes run your life,
the guilt cuts like a knife,
let me tell you what my God can do.
(my God can do)
No matter the problem,
I know Jesus He can solve them,
so hang on and He'll see you through.

Keep holdin' on, He's right beside you.
Keep bein' strong,
He'll be there to guide you.
If you should fall, don't end it all,
keep holdin' on.

You're feeling all alone,
you say from here, where do I go?
I know someone who'll make your life new oh yes He will..
You say you want to die,
first give this a try,
call out, JESUS, and He'll come to you.

Keep holdin' on, yah keep holdin' on,
He's right beside you,
He's right there with you.
Keep bein' strong,

21

He'll be there to guide you.
And if you should fall, don't end it all,
Keep holdin' on.
Just keep holdin' on to Jesus,
He's right beside you,
He's right there with you.
Ya gotta keep bein' strong,
He'll be there to guide you.
And if you should fall,
please don't end it all,
Keep (just)
Keep (just keep)
Keep (just keep holdin')
Keep (just keep holdin' on)
Keep holdin' on."*

    I had no idea who Kevin Shorey was. I did not know he was going to be there or that he was going to sing that song -- to me. But God did. He planned it. From that moment on I said, "OK, God -- not my will -- You know what is best. I will trust You."

    That was when I started allowing Jesus to help in the healing process. You see, Jesus can heal us, but we have to ask Him -- allow Him -- to work in our life. Isaiah describes Jesus healing abilities:

    "*He was despised and rejected by men, a man of sorrows, and familiar with suffering.*

    Like one from whom men hide their faces He was despised, and we esteemed him not.

    Surely he took up our infirmities, and carried our sorrows. . .

    But he was pierced for our transgressions, He was crushed for our iniquities;

    The punishment that brought us peace was upon him, and by his wounds we are healed."

    I know that Jesus sees and understands the depth of my pain and sorrow. I know that He will stand with me throughout the entire process of healing with an open heart and open arms. There is nothing I pull out of the depths of

*Keep Holding On Words & music by David Elchler & Kevin Shorey"

my agonizing hurts and raging soul, that God has not heard, nothing He does not already understand, and He still receives me with love and grace.

Most of all Jesus understands that healing is not easy. The steps can be agonizing. He already knows that I am probably going to fail and falter along that road of healing. That is where the Holy Spirit -- the Comforter -- keeps me moving ahead. Jesus keeps right on loving me, and I think He is even pleased with me. Even in the midst of my failures, He is smiling at me. It's like learning to walk. Healing is a process. If I am falling down, that means I am trying. Understanding that made me want to really repent -- to have a change of heart, to acknowledge MY sin -- and to turn from it and back to God.

Let me make one thing real clear here, I have not arrived. I still mess up. I still make bad choices. I still fall down and God still has to reach down and pick me up. But I now admit it when I fall, and I purposely look up for His hand and reach out and take hold of it. I rely on His strength and wisdom to guide me. I know no matter how many times I fall, He will ALWAYS be there to help me stand back up and begin again.

There is a song that was written by Steve Siler, Scott Krippayne and Tony Wood, and then sung by Greg Long, that captured my heart and speaks to where I am today, and how I see my connection to my most awesome heavenly Father.

I Cannot Hide From You*

Verse 1

You have looked into my heart;
You know everything about me,
You see my deepest thoughts,
And every corner of my soul,
Each single step I take,
And all my words before I speak them,
Every place that I have been
And every place that I will go.

Chorus

I cannot hide from You;
You know me all too well,
There's no story of my life
That Your memory could not tell.
I can ride the morning wings

'Til I'm completely out of view,
but, whether in dark or light,
I cannot hide from You.

Verse 2

Long before I drew first breath,
You already knew my secrets,
You watched as I was formed,
Out of sight from human eyes.
Your Spirit is with me,
And I am always in Your presence,
When I sit and when I stand,
When I sleep and when I rise.

Chorus

I cannot hide from You;
You know me all too well,
There's no story of my life
That Your memory could not tell.
I can ride the morning wings
'Til I'm completely out of view,
but, whether in dark or light,
I cannot hide from You.

Bridge:

Turn my heart from wicked ways,
Search the whispers of my mind.
And lead me on the road
That will take me home
To everlasting life!

Chorus

I cannot hide from You
You know me all too well,
There's no story of my life
That your memory could not tell.
I can ride the morning wings
'Til I'm completely out of view,
but, whether in dark or light,
every moment of my life,
I cannot hide from You.*

*I Cannot Hide From You: Words and music by: Steve Siler, Scott
Krippayne and Tony Wood

Chapter 5

The Beginning of Healings

I guess I did not really face and release my emotions -- my feelings about everything - - until about 16 years ago. After my daughter finally came to live with me; I had a hard time dealing with a 16-year-old girl, going on 21-year-old passionate woman. I still remembered her as a little 13 year old. Memories came in like a flood, and anger over lost years with her overwhelmed me. I felt cheated and did not know how to deal with her or my feelings.

I still had not dealt with all the emotions that were eating away at me. In Chuck Swindoll's book, "Starting Over" he said:

"To start over, you have to know where you are. To get somewhere else, it's necessary to know where you're presently standing."

To move on and see true healing take place, you have to know where you are with your emotions. You have to identify hidden feelings. I do not believe we can honestly do that by ourselves. Only with God's help can we see past the shame, anger, and lies, to truly identify what we are feeling and why. By facing them, owning up to the worst, we rob Satan of the power to use those feelings to keep us focused on the hurt and pain. I do not think you can ever *erase* the past, but all the pain and hurt and wreckage that goes along with it, can be healed as it is faced and released.

So I was right back at the beginning, trying to figure out "How did I get here?" This time I went to a Christian counselor.

I want to stop here and go back to the diagnosis that the specialist at the state mental hospital ended up giving me. DID/MPD: *Dissociative Identity Disorder/Multiple Personality Disorder.* The specialists, like so many in this field, believe the mind is also the home of our personalities. We all have many different aspects to our personality. One part is better able to cope with serious issues; another part is able to handle humor and less serious issues. Another part may be able to cope with sorrow and pain, while yet another part may have difficulty handling reality and is better able to function in a make-believe world. Most people are aware of these different aspects of their personality. Since it is believed that sometimes, due to trauma or abuse or maybe a stressful situation, a person's personality can fracture. There is a lot of controversy in medical science field as to whether in those incidences the main personality is unaware of the fractured personality or not.

I believe, we, as human beings are a lot like the trinity. We have a body, a soul, which includes our mind, and a spirit. When God first created us, He never intended for us to see evil or to be hurt or tormented by evil. But, being omniscient He created our minds to be self-preserving. Proverbs 27:12 says:

A prudent man sees evil and hides himself, the naive proceed and pay the penalty. New American Standard Bible

If a five-year-old child is abused and is unable to process the abuse, the mind can compartmentalize the abuse. Put it aside, as if it did not happen, to be processed at a later date. Now if that same five-year-old child at a later date surrenders his or her life to Jesus Christ; God, Jesus and the Holy Spirit can bring that abuse back from the hidden compartment to be revisited – to be processed – and for healing to take place.

Was the DID/MPD diagnosis accurate? I don't know. What I do know is I found freedom working with the Christian Counselor to reprocess the things that had happened to me. I forgave myself when I finally honestly faced all the things that had been done to me. I did not excuse it or my subsequent behavior after the fact. I just owned up to it under honest judgment. I looked at it full in the face, called it what it was -- let the horror and shock wash over me, then I turned and fell into Jesus' loving arms and let Him wipe away all the tears, and love me. And since He forgave me, I could forgive myself and everyone involved. I sometimes still cry over that wonderful feeling of peace that I felt – still feel – the receiving of God's forgiveness. That happened when I acknowledged my own sin and fell into Jesus' arms. What a safe place to be. God's forgiveness through Jesus Christ means **MY PAST IS GONE!!!!!!!** Gone, forgiven, thrown into a sea of forgetfulness -- never to be remembered again. What freedom!

I wrote out on paper everything, from my earliest memories, read through it with the Christian counselor, and then took the pages home and burned them. What a release; all gone. Oh, Satan every now and then tries to make me pick up the feelings of guilt and shame, but I just have to tell him to get away in the name of Jesus. Off he goes - so cool. What a great Protector Jesus is. By writing everything down and then going over it with the born again Christian counselor, I was better able to gain God's perspective on my wounds. I love Romans 8:28.

"And we know that God causes all things to work together for good to those who love God, to those who are called according to His purpose."
New American Standard

We can get caught up in self pity and ask the question, "Why God, why did YOU let this happen to me?" Or, we can know that although Satan meant to use this to cause our eternal destruction, God can take it and make it work all together for our ultimate good and to bring glory and honor to Him. How wonderful, that He can turn my self-destructing life into a glorious testimony of His love and power and compassion! Because of His love I am able to see other peoples' pain and know and understand just what they are feeling. My story shows there is a way to move through the pain and sorrow with God and have a life of joy.

I think the toughest thing I still have to deal with is finding the will to forgive myself. Sometimes this can be very hard, especially if I find myself making the same mistakes over and over again. I MEAN how thick is my head? Maybe I should rephrase that; "How thick is my heart?" I have found when I get my eyes off Jesus, I go into repeat mode and make the same mistakes again.

When I make the same mistakes over and over, it is easy to refuse to forgive myself. But when I do that, I leave myself open and vulnerable to attacks from Satan.

He is just waiting to whisper in my ear, "Screwed up again, didn't you? How many times do you think God is going to forgive you?" Then I start doubting God's forgiveness. I usually go to one of two extremes: whipping myself over and over for screwing up again, or I minimize in

27

my own mind my sin/mistake. Neither helps bring me back to my healing. When I finally ask Jesus to help me honestly look at my sin, and then accept God's forgiveness through Jesus, I can ask for insight on my inner makeup and needs, and then make a decision to forgive myself. I ask Jesus to help me to learn from this and to lean on Him so I do not have to go there again.

It was during a major repeat screw-up that the verses in Jeremiah 29:11-13 became real and alive in my heart and life. Genesis 2:18 says:

> **"Yahweh God said, "It is not good that the man should be alone;**
> **I will make him a helper suitable for him."**
> **World English Bible**

My heart said that it is not good for woman to be alone. It had been almost 12 years since my husband and I had separated and divorced. During all that time, I had hoped to meet someone else with whom to spend the rest of my life. The churches I attended during that time did not offer me the opportunity to meet eligible men, so I looked elsewhere.

I could probably give a whole list of reasons for what I did; tired of being alone, over-worked, lonely, empty-nest, what ever. The bottom line is that I had yet again let sin into my life and plunged rebelliously ahead to try and get what I wanted, what I deserved, even if it was not what God wanted for me! I wanted it, and that was all that mattered.

Chapter 6

Rebellion = Foolish Choices

Remember how I said that one of Satan's tricks is too white-wash our sin so it does not feel so bad? Yeah, I fell for that one, again. Women want to be loved and nurtured so badly, they will settle for something less than what they have hoped and dreamed for, believe a lie, and do almost anything. Again, I am not excusing what I did. I take full responsibility. I just want you to see just how slick Satan works and to understand just how wonderful God is when we invite Him in to overpower the deceiver. Forewarned -- forearmed!

After a rather difficult winter in 1999 and a very disappointing spring in 2000, I received a phone call from an old neighbor. This was the same neighbor whom, only thru the prayers of my daughter, I had been kept from repeating the same mistake/sin I had with my ex-husband: intimacy without the benefit of marriage, fornication. I was puzzled by his call, because we had not kept in touch after I had moved.

He told me he had remarried after I had moved away, but now the marriage was failing. He was wondering how I was doing. Said he had always admired me for my faith in God, and was trying to take a look at his life. Get back on track with his godly upbringing and the "man upstairs."

WOW! He was coming to ME for help? Visions of "saving" this man, who only wanted to be "the man" - to lavish love and affection and care on a woman, filled my heart with hope. I encouraged him to get hooked up with a good church that preached "the Word of God" and to surrender his life and will to God's direction. I sympathetically listened to all his troubles, how his wife had cheated on him and stole from him -- this kind, loving, generous man. I even encouraged him to try and get his wife to go to church with him and to see a marriage counselor. After all, we are serving the God who is in the business of restoring broken relationships, are we not?

Sounds good, doesn't it? To this day, whenever I have cause to reflect on this period of time in my life, I still shake my head in utter amazement. I now get this mental picture of Satan sitting on my shoulder, whispering in my ear, "Here is a man who is searching for God! And he came to YOU! You're doing a great job giving him direction, all those Scripture that you look up for him. You are really trying to help him and his wife. You cannot help it if she does not want to do it God's way! You are doing so much to help him and keep him on track; maybe God's reward to you will be, if his wife won't come around -- well, maybe you get the wonderful guy!"

My grandmother had a saying, "Two wrongs do not make a right." No matter how you look at it, I was going at this all the wrong way. I should not have been the person giving him counsel. If he had truly been looking for help with his marriage and with getting closer to God, he would have sought out a minister, and at the very least, I should have pointed him in that direction.

I really did pray that God would restore the marriage, but I also waited anxiously for the call from him saying the divorce was final. I had high hopes for *our* relationship. We were spending more and more time together. He came to church with me. He would come over and I would fix him a good old-fashioned home-cooked meal. We talked, and talked, and talked. We debated spiritual things - differences in beliefs. We played Scrabble and Rummy and laughed - and I smiled a lot.

I tried not to think about the differences in our beliefs. My heart filled with hope as he talked about the different things he thought should be done to improve the value of my house. Always hinting how things would be if we got together; often throwing out the question, "I wonder where we would be today if we had gotten together before?" The more time we spent together, the stronger the physical attraction became. I liked that he hinted that "he wanted me", but I really did want him to want me the way God's Word said it should be.

I tried to get him to feel sorry for me, for all the abuse I had gone through in my life, trying to manipulate him into doing the right thing. I guess I did not learn my lesson the first time that manipulation just does not work, even if you are doing it to get a right result. I think I really understand "free will" a lot better now. God gave Adam and Eve free will in the garden, even before they ate from the forbidden tree. He had to. I mean, what kind of a relationship could you have with someone who only loves and worships and obeys you because they do not have any other choice? Is it really love you are experiencing if someone only loves you because they have no other option? What's really sad about all of this is I allowed *myself* to be manipulated again. Remember what I said earlier about women wanting to be loved and nurtured? How they will settle for something less than what they have hoped and dreamed for, believe a lie, and do almost anything? Been there, done that. He used some of the standard "lines": "I don't see this relationship moving toward a commitment without going to the next level.", "It's not like we were kids and don't know what we're doing!"

Do not misunderstand me; I made the choices I made all by myself. I take full responsibility for my actions and choices. But at the time I was a little "mad" at God. I still believed the lie that Satan whispered in my heart. How could God let this man make me have to choose? Hadn't I been working so hard all this time to help him? Hadn't I prayed for his marriage? Wasn't my reward supposed to be that he would want to serve God and be the kind of husband that God's Word spoke about? My heart hardened with anger and rebellion. I deserved to have someone love me and want to be with me and take care of me!

So I made my choice again.

Chapter 7

Mercy and Peace – The Joy of Forgiveness

There is truth in the statement: "there is pleasure in sin for a season", but when God is chasing after you, the season is VERY short. And the "pleasure", well, when you know in your heart of hearts it is sin, the pleasure just is not as sweet as you had hoped it would be.

It was not long until I found myself standing alone, frustrated and hurt, filled with a deep sense of shame and regret at once again making the same mistakes and wrong choices. I felt a desperate longing for the still waters and green pastures of Psalms 23. I was tired. Tired of disappointing God; tired of the vicious circle of actions and choices I seemed to be trapped in; tired of trying to do what I wanted, what I thought was best for me; tired of not trusting God.

As these feelings of regret, shame and hopelessness washed over me, I opened my Bible.

"For I know the plans I have for you," declares the Lord, "Plans to prosper you and not to harm you, plans to give you hope and a future. Then you will call upon me and come and pray to me, and I will listen to you. You will seek me and find me when you seek me with all your heart."
Jeremiah 29:11-13 NIV

I think that is when my will finally broke. I must have read it through a dozen times. Slowly God engraved it into my heart and into my understanding. Regret and shame threatened to overwhelm me, but that's when God took me into His loving arms and filled me with the quiet assurance that He had never lost track of me, and He loved me.

To forgive yourself, you have to forgive others. To BE forgiven, we have to forgive others. Jesus talked about judging and forgiveness. He said in Matthew 7:1-2,

"Don't judge, so that you won't be judged. For with whatever judgment you judge, you will be judged; and with whatever measure (of forgiveness that) you measure, it (forgiveness) will be measured to you.
World English Bible

Jesus has really helped me to understand the importance of forgiving the people that hurt me so that I can forgive myself, thus freeing myself from one of Satan's most entangling snares. If he, Satan, can keep us entangled in the web of guilt and shame, we can never move on to all that God has for us.

I think the most important thing to understand about forgiving others is that forgiving someone else does not change them. Forgiving others changes us. It frees us from the past and from the need to try to seek revenge. Holding on to hidden hates and anger not only affects us but also, sooner or later, will affect any other relationship we may try to have. An unforgiving spirit eventually produces a very bitter person. Bitterness will spill over into our relationships, even with someone we love. In the end it is not the pain and hurt of the past that will destroy us – it is bitterness. I know this to be true - it almost destroyed me.

Once I was finally able to let go of all the past, once I gave it to Jesus, I was able to forgive those responsible for the wounds, the evil things that were done to me. I was then able to really forgive myself for all the things I did out of that pain and hurt. With that forgiveness I was able to find freedom at last from the pain, the hurt, broken life and broken promises.

God is still restoring me to wholeness. I still make mistakes, some are repeats, but that is happening less and less. The more I focus on Jesus and the fact that He has a better plan, the more I find myself leaning on Him and trusting Him. Sometimes, when I think I know better, He gently rebukes me - then I feel His love pulling me back and I turn and run to Him!

I believe He is also enabling me to bring healing to other people's lives. I truly believe that the God of hope and mercy is in the business of taking broken people and putting them back together again. Better than they were to begin with.

I believe more than anything else, God loves to take broken, flawed vessels, make them new, and then use them for His honor and glory.

I guess what I hope you will get from all of this is that no matter where you find yourself on the pathway of life, it is never too late to begin again with God. I know from first hand experience if we will truly surrender to Him, saturate ourselves in His Word, spend time literally on our knees before Him and discipline ourselves by guarding our thoughts and heart, we can rest in the promise that He will never forsake us. We may not always understand the way His hand moves in our lives, but we can rest, assure that He and He alone knows the first from the last. He will work all things out for our good, even if we do not see it immediately.

We have a choice. We can mire around in the past, in all the pain and hurt -- listen to the enemy of our soul, because that is the real battle going on here. Lose the battle for our eternal soul by believing all his lies, or we can let the joy of the Lord be our strength.

We can give all our hurts to Him. We can give up our right to have someone pay for all the bad that happened to us – we can forgive and let go. The person who will benefit, who will be totally healed, will be me. But we have to truly desire that healing. We have to truly repent and have a change of heart. We have to desire a relationship with Jesus above everything else. If you step back and look at the big picture, instead of focusing on one tiny little part, you will see that in the scope of eternity, our relationship with Jesus is all that really matters. But that choice, that decision is ours and ours alone. But we do have the choice. It is there within our grasp.

You can begin again! Our God is the God of new beginnings, of second chances. I changed some of the words in this song; words and music written by Larnelle Harris and Dave Clark. I feel God gave me the words, because it's the story of my life:

"Alone again, in a crowded room,
haunted by the questions in my mind.
It's so hard to understand,
how the life that I had planned,
stole my joy and left me far behind
Though all I had, is lost it seems,
from the shadow of a life that used to be.
I can look beyond the skies,
deep into my Father's eyes,

and see that there is hope in Christ for me.
~
I can begin again,
with the faith of a little child,
my heart has caught a vision,
of a life that's still worthwhile.
I can reach out again,
far beyond the hurt and pain,
with Your arms around me Jesus,
life will never be the same,
for new beginnings are not just for the young.
~
I face the dawn, of each brand new day,
free from all the doubt that gripped my past.
For I've found in trusting Him,
every day life starts again,
as I work toward the things that really last.
~
I can begin again, with the faith of a little child,
for my heart has caught a vision
that my life is still worthwhile.
And I can reach out again,
far beyond my hurt and pain,
with Your arms around me Jesus,
my life will never be the same,
for new beginnings are not just for the young.
New beginnings are not just for the young.
No, new beginnings are not just for. . . . the young."

Trust His heart. He won't let you down.

"The New Beginning"

*words changed slightly from original song - see original lyrics in appendix *

Appendix:
*I Can Begin Again
words and music by Larnelle Harris and Dave Clark

Alone again, in a crowded room
Cornered by the questions in my mind
It's so hard to understand
How the life that I had planned
Stole my joy and left me far behind.
Though all I have is lost it seems
From the shadow of a dream that used to be
I can look beyond the skies
Deep into the Father's eyes
And see that there is hope for one like me.
Chorus:
I can begin again
With that passion of a child
My heart has caught a vision
Of a life that's still worthwhile
I can reach out again
Far beyond what I have done
Like a dreamer who's awakened
To a life that's yet to come
For new beginnings are not just for the young.
I face the dawn
Of each brand new day
Free from all the doubt that gripped my past
For I've found in trusting him
That everyday life starts again
As I look toward the things of life that last.
(Repeat chorus twice)
Starting all over again
Is not just for the young
No matter what you've been told
It's not just for the young
It's not just for the young.